♥

||||||||||||||||||||||||||||||||||
D0039080

Important Warning:

DRINKING EXCESS ALCOHOL CAN DAMAGE YOUR HEALTH.

The publisher urges care and caution in the pursuit of any of the activities represented in this book. This book is intended for use by adults only. The publisher cannot accept any responsibility for the result of the use or misuse of this book or any loss, injury or damage caused thereby.

♠

Contents

Introduction

Most of these games have one thing in common: they combine a full glass of booze with making a complete fool of yourself – all the ingredients for a great night, in fact! These games take different formats – cards, chance, verbal, etc. – but the outcome is always the same: players will find themselves laughing hysterically at each other. Each game has a list of what you will need to play – needless to say, you will need alcohol of some sort for all of them.

So gather your friends and crack open your favourite poison: it's time to play some drinking games!

Drinking Rules

Whenever you are instructed to 'take a drink' in this book, you are expected to do so with relative moderation, so make a rule about this before you begin. A good starting point is the 'two-finger rule' – where you hold two fingers to your glass and use that as a measure of how much drink to consume each time. This can apply for drinking penalties too.

It's always fun to add some extra restrictions to keep people on their toes during an evening of silliness. If you break any of the following rules, you must take a drink:

- No pointing (you can use your elbows to gesture)
- No swearing
- You must drink with the hand that you don't normally use (e.g. your left if you are right-handed) and with your little finger pointing out.

THE MOST LIKELY TO

AMERICA

You will need:
Three or more players

Difficulty:

You'd better hope your friends think well of you!

Everyone sits in a circle around the room. Going around the circle one at a time, each player asks a 'most likely' question. For example, who is most likely to be mistaken for the Queen? Or, who is most likely to be arrested for bad behaviour? On the count of three, everyone points to the person they think best fits the bill. Players take a drink for every person pointing at them. The game continues in this way. Simple but effective!

WHAT'S
DRINKING?
A MERE PAUSE
FROM THINKING!

LORD BYRON

SHOT ROULETTE

CANADA

How to Play

You will need:
Three or more players
A variety of alcohol
Shot glasses
An empty glass bottle

Difficulty:

Spin the Bottle for grown-ups!

Place a bottle in the middle of the table so that it is lying down. This will be used as a spinner. Arrange the shot glasses in a circle around the bottle and fill with a range of different drinks. Each player takes it in turn to spin the bottle and must drink whatever the bottle chooses!

SEVEN

CHINA

You will need:
Three or more players

Difficulty: 🥃🥃

Do you remember your seven times table?

Start your game of Seven by sitting in a circle. Go around the circle counting but skipping over the number seven – so six goes to eight – because, in China, seven is considered an unlucky number. As the game goes on it gets harder as multiples of seven have to be avoided too – 14, 21, 28 and so on... Every time someone gets it wrong, they must take a drink and the game begins again at one.

CUBAN JENGA

CUBA

How to Play

You will need:
Two or more players
A set of Jenga blocks
A marker pen

Difficulty: 🥃🥃

Are you Havana a good time?

The Cubans love to drink, so get ready to have some real fun! This game involves Jenga blocks, on which you write penalties - or even dares - before starting. For example: 'stand on one leg for 30 seconds', 'write a 500-word status on Facebook', or 'suck an ice cube for one minute'. It's just like your usual family game of Jenga, but every time the tower is knocked over the guilty person must take a drink. Every time a penalty or dare is pulled out of the tower the player must do it or they have to finish their drink. Of course, the Cubans play this with shots of rum, or, at the very least, a mojito.

TOPS TOURNAMENT

SWEDEN

How to Play

You will need:

Three or more players
Cups
A permanent marker
Plastic counters or bottle tops

Difficulty: 🥃🥃

Crazy Cups!

Use the permanent marker to write all the players' names on the cups, one name per cup. Fill the cups with an equal amount of alcohol and place the cups in the middle of the floor or on a table - wherever you choose to play. Then gather around the cups in a wide circle, all players an equal distance away from the cups. Go around the circle, taking it in turns to 'challenge' one another by throwing a plastic counter or bottle top into someone else's cup. That person must then retaliate by throwing their counter or bottle top into the challenger's cup, and this continues until one of them misses. The person who misses then has to drink the contents of their cup, refill it and then challenge another player. If a player throws their counter or bottle top into their own cup they must drink up, refill and try again. If you really want to make things interesting, you can add a nameless cup to the game. Place it in the middle with all the other cups and fill it with a mixture of everyone else's drinks. If someone's top lands in this cup, they have to down the contents!

How to Play

You will need:
Three or more players
A large glass
Beer (or other drink of choice)
Vodka

Difficulty: 🥃🥃🥃🥃

Beware! Play at your own risk...

To play, fill the glass with your drink of choice. The Russians traditionally use beer (don't fret, the vodka comes later!). Stand in a circle and pass the glass around. Each player must take a drink and then replace what they have drunk with the same amount of vodka. Eventually, the glass will be completely filled with vodka and the game starts again in reverse, with the players replacing the vodka that has been drunk with beer.

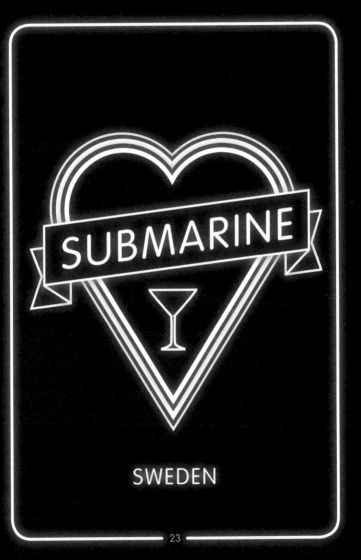

SUBMARINE

SWEDEN

How to Play

You will need:
Four or more players

Difficulty: 🥃🥃🥃

Sonar drinking.

All players sit in a circle. As submarines are underwater, players must do the following: holding both hands stretched out in front of your face, make the A-OK sign. Everyone makes a 'SHHHH' sound as the submarine dives down, and brings their A-OK signs to their eyes to show that they are now underwater. Now the game may begin.

Each player takes it in turns to say 'BOOP' to copy the sounds of a submarine's sonar. One 'BOOP' means the game carries on around the circle. When someone says, 'BOOP-BOOP' this means the next person must skip a go and stay silent. If someone chooses to mimic the sound of the submarine turning around, 'WHOHOO-HOO', then the direction of play changes. Anyone found to be making a mistake must take a drink.

DUDO

MEXICO

How to Play

You will need:

Two or more players

At least two dice (the more dice, the more challenging)

A cup

Difficulty: 🥃

Liar, liar, pants on fire!

This game is usually played with five dice, but it is completely up to you – or up to however many dice you have lying around the house. Take it in turns to be the roller. The roller puts the dice in a cup and shakes it, then takes a look inside and announces how many of the dice have rolled the same number (for example, five sixes). It is up to the roller to decide if they lie or not – however many same-number dice there are, that is how many fingers the penalty drink is worth.

The rest of the players then each state whether they think the roller has lied or not. If one of them says that the roller has lied and the roller is indeed found to be telling a fib, then the roller must take a drink (in this case, it would be five fingers' worth). However, if the roller was telling the truth, then the player to call them a liar takes a drink (again, of five fingers).

ALL IS FAIR IN LOVE AND BEER.

ANONYMOUS

2
♠

EASY-PEASY
GAMES

2
♠

You will need:
Two or more players
A clock/watch

Difficulty: 🥃

A real no-brainer.

This is possibly the easiest game in the book. Players decide how long (in minutes) the game will last – a recommended duration is five minutes – then each person picks a number from one to twelve. When the second hand of the clock/watch passes a player's chosen number, they take a drink. It's as simple as that!

How to Play

You will need:
Two or more players
A TV

Difficulty: 🥃

This one won't make your eyes go square, but it may make them a bit fuzzy.

Choose a TV show and invent some rules that dictate when players should drink. For example:

- Whenever a given character says their catch-phrase, take a drink
- Whenever you see a scene in a pub, take a drink
- Whenever you see a certain item of clothing, hair colour, accessory, animal – take a drink!

How to Play

You will need:

Two or more players
Vodka (or any other clear spirit)
Shot glasses
Water

Difficulty:

Are you feeling lucky, comrade?

Fill as many shot glasses as there are players with water, except for one, which should be filled with vodka (or your other clear spirit). Mix up the glasses and hand out the shots. Every-one must down their shot at the same time: whoever gets the vodka (the person with an unhappy look on their face and probably demanding a glass of water!) loses and is out of the next round. Repeat until there is one player left: they are the winner and can choose a drinking penalty for the other players.

THE PEANUT RACE

How to Play

You will need:
Two or more players
A bag of peanuts

Difficulty: 🥃

Not recommended for people with a nut allergy or for those who are fussy about having salty bar snacks unceremoniously plopped into their drink!

Each player drops a peanut into their own full glass at exactly the same time when someone shouts 'Drop!' The peanut will sink to the bottom, then rise up again. The player whose peanut comes to the surface last is the loser and must drink their entire glass. The loser's glass is then refilled and another round is played. After each round, players must retrieve the peanut from their glass, eat it and take another one.

I ONLY TAKE A DRINK
ON TWO OCCASIONS:
WHEN I'M THIRSTY
AND WHEN I'M NOT.

BRENDAN BEHAN

How to Play

You will need:
Three or more players

Difficulty:

No secret password required.

This one is best played on a pub crawl, while walking between pubs, but you can have a go at home if you're not too precious about your furniture! The rules are simple: if someone shouts 'Tree house!' everyone must get themselves (both feet) off the ground, e.g. up onto a step, a bench, a wall or, if you're feeling adventurous, a tree. The last person to do so must buy the next round or, if you're playing at home, down their drink.

For a sillier twist, why not change the trigger word or even make it a phrase such as 'I like turtles!' or 'Rubber baby buggy bumpers!'

3 ♦

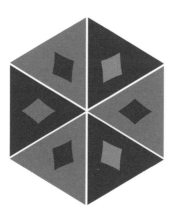

CARD GAMES

**NB: NATURALLY, ALL GAMES REQUIRE
A PACK OF PLAYING CARDS**

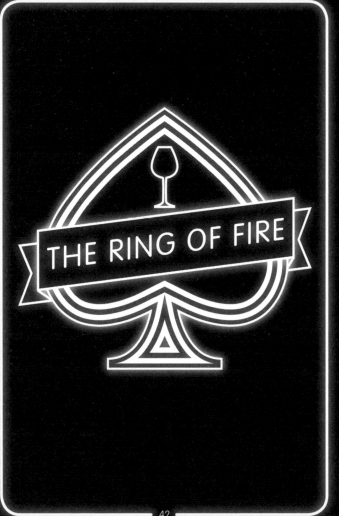

You will need:

Three or more players
An empty pint glass

Difficulty: 🥃🥃🥃🥃

Prepare to feel the burn! (If you're playing with spirits, that is.)

All players must sit in a circle, with the empty pint glass in the centre. Make the 'Ring of Fire' by spreading the cards face down around the glass. Players then take it in turns to select a card and follow the instructions below accordingly:

Black ace - nominate another player to take a drink (one finger).
Red ace - player takes a drink (one finger).
2, 3 or 4 - follow the same pattern as above from two up to four fingers.
5 - player puts their hand in the air - last player to follow suit must take a drink.

6 – player discreetly places their thumb on the table – last player to likewise do so must take a drink.

7 – the player to the left must take a drink.

8 – the player to the right must take a drink.

9 – player says a word and each player around the circle must say a word that rhymes with it. The first player to hesitate or make a mistake must drink.

10 – player nominates someone else to drink.

Jack – player must finish their drink.

Queen – everyone drinks 'to the Queen'.

King – player pours the remainder of their drink into the pint glass.

The player who picks up the fourth King must pour the remainder of their drink into the pint glass, get up onto the table, cry 'I'm king of the world!' then down the drink.

How to Play

You will need:
Three or more players

Difficulty: 🥃🥃

This is an old favourite with a boozy twist.

For this game, the more players the better. Nominate one person to be the dealer for the first round – the role then passes to the left after each round. The dealer begins by placing cards, face up, one after the other, in a pile, calling out the number of each card as they do so. When two cards of the same number come up in sequence, the first person to bring their hand down onto the top of the pile and shout 'Snap!' gets the top card; this gives them the power to nominate a player to drink a number of fingers of their drink equal to the number of the card. A round ends when the dealer has no more cards.

I'D RATHER HAVE A
BOTTLE IN FRONT OF ME
THAN A FRONTAL LOBOTOMY.

DOROTHY PARKER

HORSE RACES

How to Play

You will need:

A maximum of four players, a mimimum of two

Difficulty:

Pony up and prepare to do some drinkin'!

Remove the aces from the pack and then lay five to ten cards face down in a row, end to end (the more cards, the longer the game) – this is the 'racing track'. Place the aces (your respective 'horses') in a row perpendicular to (but one card space below) the track to create a broken 'L' shape.

Players must then name the 'horse' that they think will win, and bet a number of fingers of their drink on the horse – the more you bet, the more you can dole out for other players to drink.

How to Play

Things can get pretty heated in the world of gambling, so make a note of everyone's bets at the start of the game! When all bets have been raised, the dealer takes the rest of the pack and turns over the top card.

Whichever suit the card is, the ace of the same suit is moved forward one place along the track. The dealer continues in this manner until one horse wins the race by reaching the last card of the track.

The winner gets to dole out the fingers 'in the pot' to any one (or a combination) of the other players.

How to Play

You will need:
Two or more players

Difficulty: 🥃🥃🥃🥃

Hook, line and drinker.

Each player is dealt five cards and the rest of the pack is roughly spread out in the centre. The aim of the game is to make pairs, though if any players have pairs in their hand from the start they must discard them and take replacement cards from the pack.

Player one begins by choosing a card in their hand and asking another player of their choice if they have any cards of that rank. If the player in question has any cards that match the value of the one requested they must give them all to player one and drink two fingers of their drink if it's a numbered card, or three fingers if it's a picture card or an ace.

Player one may then place the pair face-up in front of them and take another turn. If player two does not have any cards of the requested rank, they reply 'Go Fish' and player one must drink a finger of their drink and pick up another card from the centre. (If the card they select makes a pair with one in their hand, they may discard the pair, but play still passes to the next player.)

Whenever a pair is laid down, all the other players must drink two fingers of their drinks. Play continues clockwise until one player gets rid of all their cards. The winner is the player who has discarded the highest number of pairs when the game ends – and they can choose a suitable forfeit for the losers.

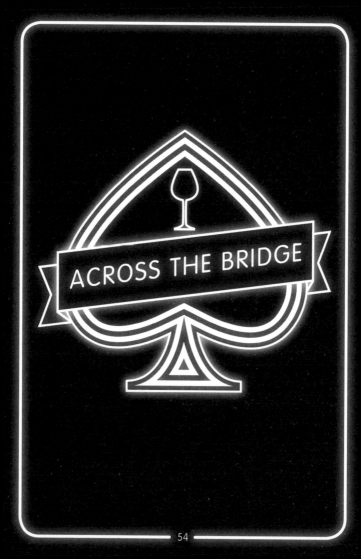

ACROSS THE BRIDGE

How to Play

You will need:
Two or more players

Difficulty: 🥃🥃🥃

This is one construction project where it's safe to drink on site.

Deal ten cards face down in a row, side by side, to form the 'bridge'. Players take turns to flip over a card; if they reveal a numbered card they're safe and play passes to the next player. If they turn over a picture card or an ace, they must drink a finger of their drink and add more cards to the bridge, depending on the card they turn over:

Jack – one finger, one card
Queen – two fingers, two cards
King – three fingers, three cards
Ace – four fingers, four cards

The game ends when all the cards on the bridge have been turned, or the pack runs out.

BEAT THE DEALER

How to Play

You will need:
Three or more players

Difficulty: 🥃🥃🥃

Beat the dealer with your card skills, not your shoe.

First, decide if aces are high or low, then cut the cards to decide who will be the dealer. The dealer holds the deck and the player to their right tries to guess the numerical value of the card on top. Without revealing it, the dealer looks at the card and tells the player whether they are right or, if not, whether it is higher or lower than their guess. The player is allowed one more attempt before the card is revealed.

The player must then drink the number of fingers' difference between their guess and the card's value. So, if the player's final guess was five and the card was an ace (low), they must drink four fingers.

How to Play

If the player guesses the card correctly on their first turn, the dealer must drink six fingers; if they guess right on their second turn, the dealer only has to drink three. Once three players have had a turn, the role of dealer passes to the next player clockwise.

The used cards are placed face up in numerical order, so that all players can see them. As more cards go out, it gets easier for players to guess correctly and beat the dealer.

ALCOHOL, TAKEN
IN SUFFICIENT
QUANTITIES, MAY
PRODUCE ALL
THE EFFECTS OF
DRUNKENNESS.

OSCAR WILDE

SPOONS

How to Play

You will need:
Three or more players
Spoons (one less than the number of players)

Difficulty: 🥃🥃

Does not involve any intimate cuddling.

Players sit in a circle with the spoons in the centre, handles facing outwards and spoon ends touching. The cards are then shuffled and four are dealt to each player. The aim of the game is to collect four of a kind (values, not suits!).

    Everyone looks at their cards, selects a card to discard and places it face down to their left, picking up the discarded card from the player on their right. This continues throughout.

Once a player has four of a kind they can take a spoon from the centre and then resume playing as before, but always discarding the card they have just picked up so that they keep their set of four.

The person who doesn't manage to grab a spoon loses and must down their drink and sit out the next round. Play starts again with one less set of cards and one less spoon and continues until only one spoon remains – the player who ends up with this is the winner.

4
♦

GAMES OF CHANCE

4
♦

How to Play

You will need:
Two or more players
A coin

Difficulty: 🥃

This game is only half sugar and spice.

This is guaranteed to get everyone in the party spirit, and is best played in a bar that has a good shots menu, or at home with a selection of spirits.

Order a variety of shots from the bar (or, if you are at home, pour some out). Make sure that there is at least one shot per person, and that about half of them are shots that taste 'nice' (think sweet ones such as Irish cream, spiced rum, peach schnapps) and the other half are 'nasty' (think tequila, black sambuca, absinthe). Each player takes it in turns to flip the coin, guessing first whether it will land heads or tails up. If they get it right, they get to drink a shot of their choice. If they get it wrong, the other players choose for them – and it's up to them to choose whether a 'nasty' or 'nice' shot is in order!

How to Play

You will need:
Three or more players
A beer mat

Difficulty:

A game of two halves (and possibly many pints).

This is the simplest game on the planet, and therefore highly recommended for those who feel they are off it. The first player takes the beer mat and flips it into the air; if it lands face up, they may nominate someone to drink; if it lands face down, the player has to drink. Each person takes it in turns to flip the mat, with a fifty-fifty chance of either having to drink or nominate someone else. The game works best if people conspire to nominate the same player to have a drink whenever they win. You had better hope that unlucky player isn't you!

ON A ROLL

How to Play

You will need:
Two or more players
A die
Six plastic cups
A marker pen
A jug

Difficulty: 🥃

Roll up! Roll up! It's time get your drink on.

Take the plastic cups, number them one to six on their side with the marker and set them out in a row on a table. Fill the jug with an alcoholic beverage of your choice.

Players take turns to roll the die; when a player rolls a number which corresponds with an empty cup, they can fill it with as much drink as they like. Play then passes to the next person. If the cup they roll already has some drink in it, they must down the contents and then roll again. Remember when you're pouring drink into a cup that you could well be the person who ends up drinking from it!

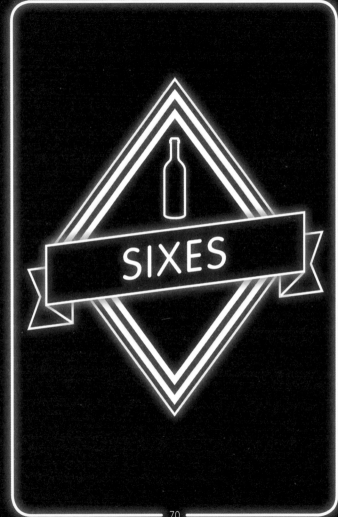

SIXES

How to Play

You will need:
Two or more players
Two dice

Difficulty: 🥃🥃

Six is the magic number.

This game is simple but effective if you have a large amount of alcohol to work your way through. Players take it in turns to roll the dice; if the numbers add up to six (for example, a four and a two) or one of them is a six, the player must drink one finger. If a player rolls a double, they must drink fingers equivalent to the number on one of the die – so if they roll a double four, they must drink four fingers. For a double three or double six, both rules apply: a finger for adding up to six, and a number of fingers for the double. So a double six means eight fingers: two for two sixes, plus another six for rolling a double six!

How to Play

You will need:

Two or more players
A plastic cup
Two dice

Difficulty: ⚏⚏⚏

Aye chihuahua!

Players take it in turns to shake the two dice in the cup and slam them down on the table. With-out letting anyone else see, the player takes a peek at what they've rolled and announces their score. Rather than adding the dice to get a score, the two numbers are combined with the highest always coming first: for example, a three and a two would make 32, a five and a four, 54, etc. A two and a one, 21, is known as a 'Mexicali' and beats all other combinations.

The aim is for each roll to be higher than the last person's; if it isn't, then players must bluff. When a player is accused of bluffing they must reveal the dice: if they were lying they must take a drink, but if they were telling the truth, the accuser must drink. If a player is caught bluffing a Mexicali, they must down their drink.

Try adding your own rules, for example:

A **61** means everyone must take a drink

A **31** means the play changes direction, etc.

A MAN'S GOT TO
BELIEVE IN SOMETHING.
I BELIEVE I'LL HAVE
ANOTHER DRINK.

W. C. FIELDS

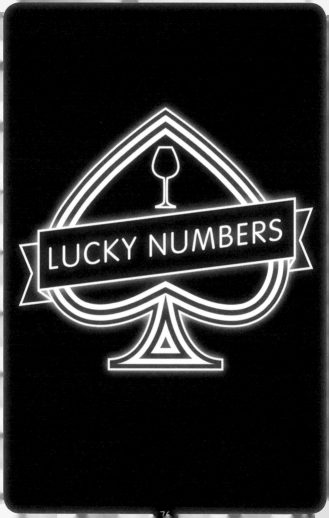

You will need:
Three or six players
A die

Difficulty:

Unfortunately, this game does not involve a grand cash prize.

Everyone chooses a number between one and six (or two numbers each if there are only three players). The first player rolls the die: whichever number it lands on, the player who chose that number must take a drink. The die is only passed on to the next player once the first player has rolled their own number and taken a drink. Simply continue until each player has had a turn at rolling the die or until you run out of drink.

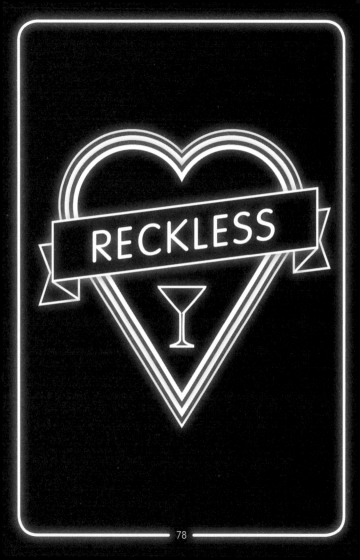

RECKLESS

How to Play

You will need:
Three or more players
A coin
An empty glass

Difficulty: 🥃🥃

Test your nerve and your drinking mettle.

Players must sit in a circle, with the empty glass in the centre. Player one takes the coin and the person to their right must pour some booze into the empty glass - the more reckless they feel, the more drink they will pour into the glass. The player doing the pouring then calls 'heads' or 'tails'. Player one must then flip the coin: if the other player has called correctly, they take the coin and play moves on, with the person to their right now adding to what's already in the glass. If they have called wrongly they must drain the glass in the centre, and player one takes another turn at flipping the coin.

5
♣

VERBAL GAMES

5
♣

THE CELEBRITY GAME

How to Play

You will need:

Two or more players

Difficulty: 🥃🥃🥃

This game will give you stars in your eyes.

Players should gather around a table or sit in a circle. Player one turns to the person on their left and says the name of a celebrity; the next player then has to think of a celebrity whose name begins with the first letter of that famous person's surname, e.g. if the first celebrity named is Aziz Ansari, the next one could be Angelina Jolie, and the next could be Jennifer Lawrence, and so on. This continues around the table; the direction will be reversed if someone says a name where the first letter of both the first name and the surname are the same, e.g. Marilyn Monroe. The most important rule is that you must play this game without pausing. If you do pause you have to 'drink while you think', drinking continuously until you think of a person. If you say a name that has already been mentioned, you have to down your drink as a penalty.

SOMETIMES
TOO MUCH TO
DRINK IS BARELY
ENOUGH.

MARK TWAIN

I HAVE NEVER

How to Play

You will need:
Three or more players

Difficulty: 🥃

Time to own up.

Players take it in turns to name something that they have never done; for example, 'I've never eaten a whole Toblerone in one sitting.' If any of the other players have done this thing (honesty is key, of course!), they must take a drink. With this game you can play to your advantage by saying things that you know the other players have done.

If any of the other players think that you are lying, they may say so and if they are right, you have to down your drink. If they are wrong the joke's on them and they have to finish their own drink!

How to Play

You will need:
Three or more players

Difficulty: 🥃🥃🥃

Do not feed the animals.

Each player must choose an animal they would like to be during the game, and an action to go with it. Before play begins everyone announces their animal and demonstrates their action – for example, if they choose to be a lion they might roar and claw the air with one hand. The sillier you make your action the better.

The first player does their animal action followed by that of any other player they choose. Play then passes to that player, who must do the animal action of the first player, their own action, and the action of another player – and so on.

Play continues until someone makes a mistake and has to down their drink, or until your sides are hurting from laughing so hard at each other doing awful animal impressions.

How to Play

You will need:
Two or more players

Difficulty: 🍶🍶🍶🍶🍶

Get into the groove. Or not.

This is one of the hardest games to play – those without a good sense of rhythm will be in trouble! Before starting the game a category has to be decided, such as 'animals' or 'film titles'. Players sit in a circle or around a table and begin the game by slapping their thighs with both hands simultaneously, then clapping their hands together and finally clicking their fingers with their left and then right hand. This routine should build up into a steady four-beat rhythm that goes: slap, clap, click, click.

Whilst the players are doing this they have to take turns to call out a word belonging to the category decided, keeping strictly to the rhythm by saying the word on the fourth beat, at the same time as the final click of their fingers. If a player fails to think of a word when the beat gets to them - or they lose the rhythm or say a word that doesn't fit the category - they must have a drink. Play continues until everyone's arms get tired.

WHO AM I?

How to Play

You will need:
Two or more players
Sticky notes
A pen or pencil

Difficulty: 🥃🥃

This is one instance where intense confusion occurs way before the hangover.

One player should write down the name of a famous person on a sticky note and stick it to the forehead of another player.

Everyone can see the name on the note except the person on whose forehead it is stuck. This person must find out who they are by asking questions to each player in turn. Only 'yes' or 'no' may be given as answers. For every 'no' given the guessing player must take a drink. Once the first player has determined who they are, play moves on. Continue until everyone's forehead is thoroughly sticky.

NOW IS THE TIME
FOR DRINKING, NOW THE
TIME TO DANCE FOOTLOOSE
UPON THE EARTH.

HORACE

SENTENCE

How to Play

You will need:
Two or more players

Difficulty: 🥃🥃🥃

Can you string one together?

Someone starts with a word – any word will do. The next person has to say a word that could help make a sentence with the word that has just been said, and so on. For example: the first person may say 'Elephants', the next may say 'like', the next 'peanuts', etc.

The game goes on until someone says a word that doesn't make sense, or until someone hesitates, or until they laugh so much that they can't talk. This person then has to have a drink and the game continues.

The sentences constructed when this game is played can become absolutely bizarre (and hilarious), especially if some of the players are lateral thinkers – but as long as the sentence makes grammatical sense, it will count.

You will need:
Three or more players

Difficulty:

Fuzzy duck? Duzzy...

Players should sit in a circle. The first player turns to their left and says, 'Fuzzy Duck'; the next person turns to their left and does the same. This continues until a player turns to the person who's just said 'Fuzzy Duck' to them, and says 'Duzzy?' The question changes the direction and the phrase to be repeated then changes to 'Ducky Fuzz'. Anyone can reverse the direction by saying 'Duzzy?', but each person may only do it twice per round.

The idea is to go around the circle as fast as you can; stalling or getting it wrong means you have to take a drink. It's probably best not to play this one within earshot of your mother-in-law/local priest/ young children.

6 ♥

SILLY GAMES

♠ 9

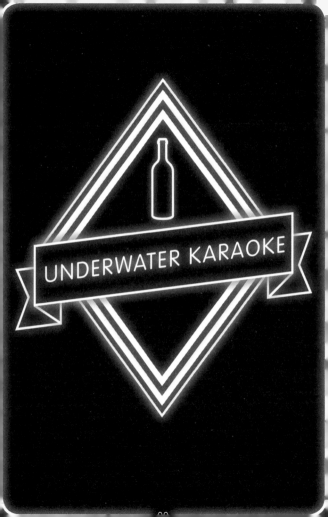

How to Play

You will need:
Three or more players

Difficulty: 🍶🍶

Check one; check two.

Each player takes it in turn to perform a song for their 'audience'. The catch is that songs cannot be sung - they must be gargled through alcoholic beverages! The other players take turns to identify the song being 'sung', and each incorrect guess is punished by a drinking penalty. If, after a second gargled rendition, none of the players can guess the tune, the performer must finish their drink.

Continue for as many rounds as your ears can bear!

ALCOHOL MAY BE MAN'S WORST ENEMY, BUT THE BIBLE SAYS LOVE YOUR ENEMY.

FRANK SINATRA

How to Play

You will need:
Three or more players
A stereo

Difficulty: 🥃🥃

Musos and booze-os unite!

One player is nominated as the DJ and the others take turns to identify songs being played. However, their guesses must come within the first five seconds of the track. If a song is incorrectly guessed after the allotted time, the player must down their drink; if a song is correctly guessed, play moves to the next person.

A player can choose to attempt identification in less than five seconds, subject to the following drinking penalties/bonuses if they get it wrong/right:

A wrong guess at four seconds – player drinks four fingers; a right guess – DJ has to drink one finger.

A wrong guess at three seconds – player drinks three fingers; a right guess – DJ drinks two fingers.

A wrong guess at two seconds – player drinks two fingers; a right guess – DJ drinks three fingers.

A wrong guess at one second – player drinks one finger; a right guess – DJ must drink four fingers!

Continue until the DJ's start/stop-track finger gets sore.

FOLLOW MY LEAD

How to Play

You will need:
Three or more players

Difficulty: 🥃🥃

The blind leading the blind.

This is a copy-cat game, but instead of a 'Simon says...' instruction, players must deduce by observation the action they must copy. Any player may choose to do an action at any time. For example: someone might decide to put their thumb on their forehead, and everyone has to follow suit. The last person to catch on has to have a drink.

How to Play

You will need:

Three or more players
Twister
Four types of alcohol

Difficulty: 🥃🥃🥃

Put your flexibility to the test!

This game is identical to a regular game of Twister except that the play is made even harder by the introduction of alcohol. Assign a different type of alcohol to each coloured circle, for example, blue could be beer. Spin the Twister dial, and when the person places their hand or foot on the circle they must also be fed a shot by the person in charge of the spinner. If a person falls they must take two shots as punishment.

How to Play

You will need:

Two or more people
A timer or a digital watch
Cups or shot glasses
Beer

Difficulty: 🥃🥃🥃

The ultimate stamina test!

This game can be played with any number of people. Line up several shots of beer for each person playing, and drink a shot every minute for 100 minutes (refill the glass after every hit). Use a watch to time yourself or simply pay attention to the clock. Try reciting tongue twisters at top speed or dancing around between shots to spice things up. The person who lasts the longest is the winner. Make sure each shot is small – the key to winning here is pacing yourself. The game can be scaled back to 50 or 25 minutes depending on the amount of time you want to spend on the game.

How to Play

You will need:

Two or more players
A snakes and ladders board game

Difficulty:

What goes up, must come down!

Play a straightforward game of Snakes and Ladders, but with the following drinking instructions:

Up a ladder – this player nominates an opponent to drink.

Down a snake – this player must have an agreed quantity of their drink.

At the end of the game, the loser(s) must down whatever is left of their drink.

How to Play

You will need:

An even number of players (four or more)
A long table
Plastic cups

Difficulty: 🥃

Scull your way to drunken victory.

Be warned: things can get really messy with this game! Divide into two teams and line up on opposite sides of a long table. Each player will need a cup filled with drink – make sure the cups are all the same size and filled to the top.

On the count of three, the first player on each team starts to drink. Once they've drained their cup, they slam it upside down onto the table, which is the signal for the next player in their team to start drinking.

If a player spills any of their drink, or turns their cup over before completely finishing it, their cup is refilled and they have to start again. The same goes for any overly keen player who starts drinking prematurely when the player before them hasn't yet finished.

The winning team is the first to have all its members finish drinking. They may then choose a forfeit or drinking penalty for the losing team.

PASS THE BUCK

You will need:

Three or more players
A stereo
A note (paper money)

Difficulty:

Easy money.

This game is similar to Pass the Parcel, but requires much less preparation. Everyone sits in a circle except for the DJ, who is responsible for playing and stopping the music. Players must pass a note around the circle; whoever is holding the note when the music stops must have a drink. If two people are touching it, mid-exchange, they must both drink. Play continues until a person has had the note stop at them three times – they are the winner and may also claim the note as their prize!

How to Play

You will need:
Four players
Two ping-pong balls
Twenty plastic pint glasses
 A long(ish) table
A 'side drink'

Difficulty: 🍺🍺🍺🍺

Prepare to get batted!

Set out the pint glasses in two sets of ten, in a triangular 4-3-2-1 formation, at each end of the table and fill them all at least half full with beer.

Players divide into two teams and position themselves at opposite ends of the table. A player from each team takes their turn to throw their ping-pong ball into any one of the glasses at the end opposite to where they are standing.

Every time a team member scores, a member of the opposite team must drink the contents of the cup the ball has landed in. The aim is to eliminate all of your opponents' cups first. If any player misses the cups completely, i.e. the ball lands on the table or on the floor, they must take a drink from their 'side drink'.

To spice things up a bit, have a few 'killer' cups in each set, containing something like whiskey, vodka or rum.

BUT I'M NOT
SO THINK AS YOU
DRUNK I AM.

J. C. SQUIRE

THE AFTER-DINNER MINT GAME

How to Play

You will need:

Two or more players
A pack of after-dinner mints (the flat, wafer-like kind)
Shot glasses

Difficulty: 🥃🥃🥃

The perfect digestif?

Each player takes an after-dinner mint and pours themselves a shot of alcohol. At the word 'Go!' players must place their after-dinner mints on their forehead and, with their hands behind their backs, attempt to get it into their mouth without touching it at all.

If a player drops their mint, they must down their shot. Play continues until you get sick of the taste of booze and minty chocolate.

How to Play

You will need:

Two or more players
A pitcher
An empty glass (not too heavy!)

Difficulty: 🥃🥃🥃

Man the lifeboats!

This nerve-wracking game will have you holding your breath as the tension mounts: be prepared to get covered in booze at some point!

Each player should have their own full glass of drink at the beginning of the game. Sit around a table, with the semi-full pitcher in the centre. Put the empty glass, upright, into the pitcher so that it floats. You may need to pour a small amount of drink into the bottom of the glass before play commences to give it some stability.

Each player then takes it in turn to pour some of their own drink into the floating glass, waiting a few seconds to see whether or not the glass sinks. Play continues in this manner until the glass finally does sink. The unlucky player who causes this to happen must fish the glass out from the bottom of the pitcher and down its contents.

HAPPY DRINKING!

If you're interested in finding out more about our books, find us on Facebook at **Summersdale Publishers** and follow us on Twitter at **@Summersdale**.

www.summersdale.com

Image credits

Assorted glasses and bottles – pp.9, 11, 12, 14, 16, 18, 21, 23, 25, 28, 30, 32, 34, 36, 39, 42, 45, 48, 51, 54, 56, 59, 60, 64, 66, 68, 70, 72, 76, 78, 81, 83, 84, 86, 88, 91, 94, 96, 99, 101, 102, 105, 107, 109, 111, 113, 116, 118, 122, 124, 127 © agrion/Shutterstock.com

Shot-glass difficulty icon (throughout)
© etraveler/Shutterstock.com

Playing-card suit vectors (throughout)
© Vitezslav Valka/Shutterstock.com

p.8 – globe © Arcady/Shutterstock.com

p.29 – cocktails © kalmil/Shutterstock.com

p.80 – Jack © Maisei Raman/Shutterstock.com

p.98 – Joker © Maisei Raman/Shutterstock.com

p.128 – glass © kalmil/Shutterstock.com